MAYER SMITH

Embers of the Forgotten Flame

Copyright © 2025 by Mayer Smith

All rights reserved. No part of this publication may be reproduced, stored or transmitted in any form or by any means, electronic, mechanical, photocopying, recording, scanning, or otherwise without written permission from the publisher. It is illegal to copy this book, post it to a website, or distribute it by any other means without permission.

This novel is entirely a work of fiction. The names, characters and incidents portrayed in it are the work of the author's imagination. Any resemblance to actual persons, living or dead, events or localities is entirely coincidental.

Mayer Smith asserts the moral right to be identified as the author of this work.

Mayer Smith has no responsibility for the persistence or accuracy of URLs for external or third-party Internet Websites referred to in this publication and does not guarantee that any content on such Websites is, or will remain, accurate or appropriate.

Designations used by companies to distinguish their products are often claimed as trademarks. All brand names and product names used in this book and on its cover are trade names, service marks, trademarks and registered trademarks of their respective owners. The publishers and the book are not associated with any product or vendor mentioned in this book. None of the companies referenced within the book have endorsed the book.

First edition

*This book was professionally typeset on Reedsy.
Find out more at reedsy.com*

Contents

1	The Return of a Ghost	1
2	Whispers in the Ashes	8
3	Beneath the Masks	15
4	A Kiss Meant to Burn	23
5	Smoke and Secrets	31
6	Dancing with the Enemy	39
7	Shattered Promises	47
8	A Trail of Ash and Lies	56
9	The Edge of Betrayal	64
10	Flames of the Past	73
11	When Fire Meets Fire	81
12	the Forgotten Flame	90

One

The Return of a Ghost

Selene Duvall never believed in ghosts. Not the kind that rattled chains in the dead of night or whispered secrets in the wind. But the man standing in the doorway of her gallery—drenched from the rain, shadows clinging to him like an omen—was undeniably a ghost.

Her ghost.

Adrian Vale.

For three years, she had mourned him. For three years, she had told herself she was foolish to still dream of the way his lips felt against hers, of the nights they spent tangled in silk sheets, of the promises he whispered against her skin. And for three years, she had tried—desperately, hopelessly—to let go of a man who no longer existed.

But now, against every law of reality, against every wound she had forced herself to stitch closed, Adrian was here. And he was staring at her as though she was the ghost.

Selene's fingers tightened around the glass of wine she'd been holding. The stem trembled in her grip, and for a second, she thought it might shatter.

She willed herself to breathe. To speak. But words failed her, strangled by the storm raging inside her chest.

Adrian hadn't moved. He stood just inside the entrance, the warm glow of the gallery's lights casting jagged shadows across his face. The storm outside still howled, sheets of rain hammering against the windows, and yet he looked untouched by it, as if he had emerged from something far darker than the night.

His dark hair was longer than she remembered, curling slightly at the edges where it had grown unruly. A faint scar slashed through his left eyebrow—a mark that hadn't been there before. And his eyes... God, his eyes.

They had always been an inferno, but now they were nothing but embers. Burnt out. Haunted.

Selene forced herself to find her voice. "You're dead."

The words barely scraped past her throat.

Adrian's lips parted slightly, but he didn't speak. He didn't

The Return of a Ghost

even blink. He only watched her, his chest rising and falling in measured breaths, as if he were calculating every possible outcome of this moment.

It made her stomach twist with something sharp and unfamiliar.

Anger.

The kind that had been simmering for three years, slow and quiet, waiting for the moment to erupt.

Her pulse thundered in her ears as she set her wine down on the counter with a sharp clink and stepped forward. The air between them felt like a wire pulled too tight, ready to snap at the slightest touch.

"I buried you," she said, voice shaking. "I mourned you. I—" She swallowed hard. "How dare you."

The words weren't enough. They barely scratched the surface of the fire roaring inside her.

Adrian exhaled slowly, but still, he didn't move.

"I had no choice." His voice was low, gravelly.

Selene laughed, sharp and bitter. "No choice? You had no choice but to disappear? To let me believe you were rotting in some godforsaken grave?"

His jaw clenched. She saw the flicker of something in his

expression—guilt, maybe—but it was gone too quickly to grasp.

She hated how familiar he still was. How, even through the fury, her body betrayed her, remembering the warmth of his touch, the way his fingers used to trace the line of her spine as if memorizing her.

She hated him for being here. For ruining everything she had spent years trying to rebuild.

Adrian finally stepped forward. Just one step. But it was enough to send a shiver down her spine.

"Selene," he said, softer now. "You need to leave the city."

She froze.

A slow, terrible chill crept through her veins.

"What?"

Adrian's gaze flickered to the large glass windows that framed the gallery, rain streaming down them like liquid silver. Then, as if sensing something in the shadows beyond, he took another step closer.

Too close.

Selene could see the storm clinging to him now—the droplets of rain darkening the fabric of his shirt, the faint tremor in his fingers before he curled them into fists.

She should have stepped back. Should have put a wall between them, something to protect herself from the onslaught of old wounds tearing open inside her.

But she didn't.

"Please," he said, and it wasn't an order. It was a plea. "You're in danger."

Selene swallowed. "You don't get to walk back into my life after three years and tell me what to do."

He exhaled sharply. "I know. But this isn't about me. If you stay here, they will come for you."

They.

The word slithered into her mind like ice.

"Who?" she demanded.

Adrian hesitated. Just for a fraction of a second. But it was enough.

"Get out," she whispered.

His entire body went still.

"Selene—"

"Get. Out."

She didn't wait for him to argue. Didn't give him the chance to feed her more cryptic warnings. She turned on her heel and stalked toward the back of the gallery, her heartbeat a war drum against her ribs.

But before she could take another step, Adrian moved.

Faster than she could react, his fingers closed around her wrist, his grip firm but not painful. The warmth of his skin against hers sent a bolt of electricity through her, memories crashing into her with the force of a tidal wave.

The nights they had spent in the dark, tangled together.
　The way he had once whispered her name like a prayer.
　The way he had held her when she thought the world was falling apart.

Now, the world was falling apart all over again.

Adrian's voice was barely more than a breath. "I never wanted to leave you."

Selene squeezed her eyes shut. "But you did."

A heavy silence stretched between them.

Then, just as quickly as he had grabbed her, Adrian let go.

She didn't turn around. Didn't look at him as he exhaled, as if resigning himself to something inevitable.

The Return of a Ghost

The door creaked open behind her, and for a moment, the wind howled through the space, cold and merciless.

Then, the door clicked shut.

Selene stood there, motionless, her heart in her throat.

Adrian Vale had returned from the dead.

And he had just walked out of her life again.

But this time, the fire he had left behind wasn't the kind that could be extinguished.

This time, it was the kind that burned.

Two

Whispers in the Ashes

The scent of smoke still clung to the air when Selene returned to the gallery the next morning. She had hoped the fog of the previous night's encounter with Adrian would have lifted, that the confusion and raw ache in her chest would have faded with the dawn. But as she stepped into the ruins of her once-beloved space, the weight of the ashes buried everything else.

Her gallery, once a sanctuary for delicate art and curated beauty, now lay in charred ruins. What should have been a space of peace felt like a battlefield. The floor was slick with soot, the walls scarred with dark streaks, the windows shattered and jagged like teeth left bared in the mouth of a beast.

Everywhere she looked, there were remnants of things she had poured her soul into—artworks she had nurtured, memories she had cherished—now reduced to nothing but cold cinders.

Selene's breath caught as she stepped further into the gallery, the acrid scent of smoke seeping into her skin. It felt like an affront, a betrayal by something she couldn't see but could feel lurking in the shadows. It wasn't just the fire that had destroyed her gallery; it was something far more insidious, something that had been creeping closer, invisible yet undeniable.

As she moved toward the counter, her fingers grazed the scorched wood, and her pulse quickened. A rustle broke the silence—the faintest whisper behind her.

She froze.

For a heartbeat, everything went still.

The air was heavy with the remnants of the fire, and the rain, which had let up in the early hours of the morning, had begun to fall once more, steady and relentless. But beneath that sound, there was something else—a whisper that tugged at the edges of her sanity.

Selene's heart pounded in her chest as she slowly turned.

There, standing near the back of the gallery, half-hidden in the shadows, was a figure. She couldn't see his face, only the outline of his form—a man, tall and impossibly still. Her mind screamed to run, but her feet betrayed her, staying planted on the ground as if by some unseen force.

"Who's there?" she demanded, her voice sharp and unnerving in the silence.

The figure didn't move. His presence, though silent, filled the space, oppressive and thick, like an unseen hand wrapped around her throat.

And then—his voice.

"It's not over, Selene."

Her breath caught, the words cutting through her like glass.

She knew that voice.

Even though it was softer now, more strained, there was no mistaking it.

Adrian.

Her chest constricted, panic rushing in like a tidal wave, and yet her feet remained frozen, unable to move, to escape the ghost of a past she had long buried.

"You shouldn't have come back," she whispered, her throat tight with emotion.

The figure shifted then, stepping into the weak light that filtered through the broken windows. The faint glimmer of morning seemed to break against him, revealing the hard edge of his jawline, the dark shadow beneath his eyes. The weariness in his movements spoke of nights without sleep, of too many days spent running, of things that hadn't been said.

Adrian stood there, staring at her as if he, too, were caught between past and present, between regret and necessity. The distance between them was like a gulf, an ocean of silent years, and yet the electricity that had always hummed between them was still there, unspoken but undeniable.

"You shouldn't be here." His words were soft, tinged with something she couldn't read. Was it fear? Was it sorrow?

"I don't know where else to go," she replied, her voice trembling despite her best efforts to stay calm. "You—you came into my life without warning, and now you want to leave again?"

Adrian closed his eyes briefly, his fingers twitching as if wanting to reach out to her, but he held himself back. "I never wanted to leave you, Selene. But this—this thing that's after us, it's bigger than both of us. You're not safe here."

Selene shook her head, her pulse still racing, her mind a whirlwind of emotions. How could he still be here, still demand her to leave? After all this time? After all the lies?

"Why did you leave me?" The words slipped out before she could stop them. She'd asked herself this question a thousand times in the years that had passed, but now, it hung in the air between them, raw and aching.

Adrian's expression darkened. "I had no choice, Selene. You

don't understand—"

"I don't understand?!" she cried, taking a step toward him despite the gnawing fear that curled in her chest. "You disappeared without a word! I thought you were dead, Adrian! And now you show up here, and you expect me to just forgive you?"

She was shaking now, tears blurring the edges of her vision, but she refused to let them fall. She couldn't afford to be weak, not now.

"I'm not asking for forgiveness," Adrian said, his voice low and hoarse. "I'm asking you to trust me."

A bitter laugh escaped her lips. "Trust you? After all of this?"

He didn't respond, just stood there, looking at her as if he were seeing her for the first time in years, his expression a mixture of longing and something darker—something she couldn't quite grasp.

"I need you to listen," he said, his voice shaking with intensity. "They're coming, Selene. Whoever did this—" He gestured to the wreckage of the gallery—"they're just the beginning. You've been dragged into something you don't understand, and I can't protect you if you stay here."

His words chilled her to the bone.

"Who are they, Adrian?" she asked, her voice barely a whisper.

For a moment, Adrian hesitated, and in that hesitation, she saw something flicker—a shadow of the man he used to be, the man she had loved. But then it was gone, swallowed by the cold, hard man standing before her.

"They're the ones who made me disappear," he said quietly. "The ones who wanted me dead. And now they know about you."

Her chest tightened, her breath shallow as the pieces began to fall into place. The fire—the broken window—Adrian's sudden reappearance—it was all connected.

But how?

Before she could ask another question, the sharp sound of footsteps echoed down the corridor.

Adrian's eyes widened. "They've found us."

Selene barely had time to react before he was pulling her toward the back of the gallery, his grip firm but not harsh. He moved quickly, like someone who knew exactly how much time they had left.

"Stay close," he ordered.

Selene's heart pounded as she followed him, her mind racing to catch up with the whirlwind of events. She didn't understand, didn't know who was after them, but there was no denying the fear in Adrian's eyes.

They weren't alone anymore.

And the danger was closer than ever.

Three

Beneath the Masks

The night air clung to Selene's skin like a second layer, thick with the scent of rain and the distant hum of the city. The cold crept into her bones as she leaned against the rusted railing of her apartment's fire escape, trying to calm the chaos spiraling inside her.

Adrian had disappeared again.

Not in the way he had three years ago—not into the abyss of the unknown, not into the whispers of death—but into the city, swallowed by shadows, promising he would return.

They're coming, Selene.

His warning refused to leave her mind. The weight of it pressed against her chest, an invisible force wrapping tight around her lungs.

Whoever "they" were, they had burned down her gallery. They had left her a message wrapped in flames, and Adrian... he knew more than he was telling her.

Her grip tightened around the metal railing.

Adrian Vale had always been an enigma—a puzzle she had once thought she could solve. Back then, she had loved him with reckless abandon, never doubting that he was her safe harbor, her forever.

But love, she had learned, wasn't always enough to keep a man from vanishing into the dark.

A gust of wind swept through the narrow alley below, carrying the scent of damp pavement and gasoline. The city was restless tonight. She could feel it in her bones, in the electric hum of something unseen, something watching.

She turned her gaze toward the apartment window, where the reflection of her own silhouette stared back at her. Inside, the room was dimly lit, golden light casting long shadows across the wooden floor. She had locked the door, checked the windows twice. But it wasn't the locks that unsettled her.

It was the feeling.

The feeling that someone had already been inside.

She swallowed hard and stepped back into the apartment, the floorboards creaking beneath her weight. Her fingers skimmed the edges of the desk, trailing over the worn wood, the stacks of papers, the half-drunk glass of wine she had abandoned hours ago.

Then she saw it.

A single envelope.

It hadn't been there before.

Her breath hitched. The paper was cream-colored, thick, and smooth beneath her fingertips. No address, no stamp. Just her name.

Selene.

She forced herself to move, to pick it up, to turn it over. The flap was already broken, as if someone had left it knowing she would find it.

Her pulse roared in her ears as she pulled out the note inside.

The handwriting was precise. Unfamiliar.

You should have left when you had the chance.

Her heart slammed against her ribs.

Selene dropped the letter as if it had burned her, her hands trembling.

Adrian had been right.

Whoever had set fire to the gallery, whoever had dragged him back into her life, was watching her.

A sudden knock at the door made her jerk back, her pulse skyrocketing.

She reached for the nearest thing she could use as a weapon—a brass letter opener—before stepping toward the door. Her breath came in shallow bursts as she pressed her palm against the wood.

"Who is it?" she called, her voice steadier than she felt.

Silence.

Then—

"It's me."

Adrian.

Her stomach twisted. He hadn't given her time to prepare, to fortify the walls she had spent years building.

She unlocked the door, letting it swing open just enough to see him. His face was half in shadow, the dim glow from the hallway catching the sharp lines of his jaw, the hollow look in his eyes.

"You're bleeding," she said before she could stop herself.

A thin line of crimson trailed from his temple down to his cheekbone, disappearing into the collar of his dark jacket.

"It's nothing," he said.

"It doesn't look like nothing."

Adrian exhaled through his nose, his gaze flicking over her, searching. For what, she didn't know.

"Can I come in?"

She hesitated. The letter on the floor still taunted her, a reminder that danger was not just a possibility—it was already here.

But Adrian was already inside before she could decide, brushing past her, his presence filling the room like a storm.

He locked the door behind him.

"You're not safe here," he said, his voice low, urgent. "They've marked you."

Selene swallowed the lump in her throat. "I know."

His brows pulled together. "What do you mean, you know?"

Wordlessly, she bent down, picking up the letter and holding it out to him. He took it, his fingers brushing hers for the briefest moment before he unfolded the paper, his eyes scanning the message.

She saw the shift in his expression—the barely contained fury, the tension tightening his jaw.

Adrian crushed the note in his fist. "Pack a bag."

Selene blinked. "Excuse me?"

"You're leaving."

She scoffed, crossing her arms. "You don't get to decide that."

Adrian stepped closer, and the sheer proximity of him sent her senses into chaos. He smelled like rain, leather, and something distinctly him—a scent she had spent years trying to forget.

"Selene," he said, softer now, but no less intense. "This isn't a game. These people—whoever they sent this—won't stop. They don't warn. They act."

A shiver ran down her spine. "Then tell me who they are. Stop hiding things from me."

He hesitated.

"Damn it, Adrian," she hissed. "You left me in the dark once. I won't let you do it again."

His chest rose and fell in a measured breath.

Then, finally—

"There's an organization. A network. One that operates beneath the surface of the city."

Selene's stomach twisted. "And you were involved."

His silence was answer enough.

She took a step back, her heart pounding. "You were lying to me, this entire time."

His hands curled into fists. "I never lied to you."

Selene let out a bitter laugh. "You let me believe you were dead, Adrian."

Something in his expression cracked.

"I did it to protect you."

She shook her head, refusing to let his words seep into her, refusing to let the pain in his eyes become her own.

"You don't get to make that decision for me," she said, voice thick with unshed emotion.

Adrian stepped forward again, closing the distance between them until there was barely an inch between their bodies.

"I need you to trust me," he murmured.

Selene's breath hitched.

His eyes burned into hers, searching, pleading.

And for a split second—just a breath—she let herself remember what it was like to love him.

But trust?

That was something she wasn't sure she could give.

Not anymore.

Four

A Kiss Meant to Burn

Selene had spent years convincing herself that Adrian Vale was nothing more than a memory. A cruel specter from the past that had haunted her through lonely nights and unanswered questions. But now, as she stood in the dim glow of her apartment with him just inches away, she felt like she was standing on the edge of a precipice, one step away from either salvation or ruin.

The air between them was thick, charged with a current neither of them could deny. The past pressed against the present, a living thing clawing its way back into existence.

But there was no time for nostalgia.

"You don't get to stand here and tell me to trust you, Adrian," she said, her voice trembling between anger and something far more dangerous. "Not after what you did."

Adrian's gaze flickered, a shadow passing over his face. "I know."

Selene hated how much those two words did to her. How they buried themselves deep in her chest, how they almost sounded like an apology.

Almost.

She turned away before he could say anything else, before she could drown in the look in his eyes.

"I'm not leaving the city," she said, forcing steel into her voice. "This is my life, Adrian. I built it from the ground up, and I won't run just because some faceless people want me gone."

Adrian ran a hand through his hair, his frustration evident. "Then you're making yourself an easy target."

Selene laughed dryly. "Do I look like I have much of a choice?" She gestured to the ruined gallery through the rain-streaked window. "They already took everything from me."

His jaw tightened. "No. They haven't."

Something about the way he said it made her chest tighten. It was a promise. A vow.

She didn't know if she could believe in promises anymore.

Before she could respond, a loud, sharp bang shattered the silence.

Selene flinched, her instincts kicking in. It took her less than a second to realize that the sound had come from outside—metal against metal, like something heavy being slammed shut.

Adrian moved before she did, reaching for the knife strapped to his belt, his body instantly coiled with tension. "Turn off the lights."

Selene didn't argue. She rushed to the nearest lamp, twisting the switch until darkness swallowed the room.

They stood there, frozen, listening.

The rain was relentless outside, drumming against the glass, but beyond that, there was something else—a presence, unseen but tangible.

Selene's heartbeat roared in her ears as she backed away from the window, instinct telling her to move away from any vantage points.

Adrian moved with precision, his body a controlled force of muscle and focus as he approached the edge of the window, careful to remain in the shadows.

Then—

A flicker of movement.

Barely there. A shifting of shadows across the alleyway.

But Selene saw it.

A figure.

Standing beneath the glow of the streetlamp, just beyond the reach of the rain, like a statue carved from the night itself.

Cold fear slithered down her spine.

Adrian exhaled sharply. "They found you faster than I expected."

Selene clenched her fists. "Who?"

Adrian didn't answer. Instead, he turned to her, his eyes burning with something fierce and unyielding. "Pack what you need. Now."

Selene stood her ground. "No."

Adrian tensed. "Selene—"

"No!" she hissed. "I'm done running blind. I want answers, Adrian! Who the hell are they?"

His eyes darkened. "The people I used to work for."

A sharp silence followed his words.

Selene felt like the air had been stolen from the room.

She knew Adrian wasn't just some ordinary man. He had always been too good at reading people, too sharp, too skilled. But she had never asked questions. Never pushed.

Because she had been in love with him.

And love, she realized now, had made her blind.

"Your work," she said slowly, voice barely above a whisper. "That's why you disappeared?"

A muscle in Adrian's jaw twitched. "Yes."

Selene took a step back, her world tilting.

He reached for her before he could stop himself, his fingers barely brushing her wrist before she yanked away.

The movement stung. More than it should have.

"I never wanted to leave you, Selene," Adrian said, his voice low, edged with something dangerously close to desperation. "I had to."

She swallowed against the emotion clawing up her throat. "And now they're after me because of you."

He didn't deny it.

Selene let out a shuddering breath, her hands shaking. "How do I know you're not part of this?"

Adrian stilled. The accusation hung between them like a blade, sharp and unforgiving.

She had expected anger. Expected him to lash out, to be offended.

Instead, he took a step closer, slow and deliberate, until she could feel the heat radiating from his body.

"You don't," he murmured. "But you do know me."

His voice was different now—softer, almost aching.

And damn him, she did.

She knew the way he breathed when he was lying. Knew the way his body tensed when he was afraid.

And right now, Adrian Vale was afraid.

Not for himself.

For her.

She hated that she believed him.

Hated that even after everything, even after years of silence and grief, he could still make her heart betray her.

Adrian reached up then, fingers brushing against her jaw so lightly it could have been mistaken for a ghost of a touch.

"Selene," he whispered.

Her pulse stuttered.

She should have pulled away. Should have stepped back.

But she didn't.

She let him touch her. Let him tilt her face toward his.

And when he leaned in, when his lips hovered just above hers, a breath apart, she felt the burn of it—of everything they had lost, everything that had been taken from them.

And then—

The glass shattered.

A bullet tore through the window, embedding itself in the opposite wall.

Selene's scream was muffled by Adrian as he grabbed her, pushing her down just as another shot rang out.

The apartment was plunged into chaos, the rain roaring through the broken window as more glass splintered onto the floor.

Adrian's body was heavy against hers, shielding her from whatever was outside.

"Stay down," he ordered, his voice raw.

Selene could barely breathe. Could barely process what had just happened.

But one thing was clear.

This wasn't a warning.

Whoever they were, they weren't planning to let her walk away alive.

Five

Smoke and Secrets

Selene's ears rang, a sharp, disorienting sound that blurred the edges of her reality. The scent of gunpowder and shattered glass thickened the air, mingling with the damp, metallic bite of rain sweeping in through the broken window. Adrian's weight was still pressed against her, solid and protective, his breath ragged against her temple.

"Stay low," he ordered, his voice a quiet demand as he shifted off her.

Selene's pulse thundered in her ears, but she forced herself to move. The wooden floor was littered with glass shards, reflecting broken slants of light from the flickering streetlamp outside. The room felt smaller now, suffocated by the echoes of gunfire, by the heavy presence of the unseen threat lurking in the darkness beyond the window.

Adrian's movements were sharp, methodical. He reached for his weapon—she barely saw the sleek glint of metal before he was up, pressing his back against the wall beside the window, his body coiled tight like a predator on the verge of striking. His gaze flicked to her.

"Are you hurt?"

Selene shook her head, even though she wasn't entirely sure. Her heart was still galloping in her chest, her nerves raw and frayed.

"What the hell just happened?" she whispered, her voice hoarse.

Adrian's expression darkened. "They found us."

The words sent another rush of cold through her veins.

They.

Whoever they were, they weren't just watching anymore. They had acted.

She swallowed hard. "Do you see them?"

Adrian's jaw tightened as he risked a glance through the jagged remains of the window. Rain dripped from the shattered edges, the wind howling through the opening like a living thing.

Selene could see the tension in the set of his shoulders, in the way his fingers flexed around the gun.

Then—so quickly she barely registered the movement—he fired.

A single shot. Sharp. Precise.

A grunt of pain echoed from below.

Selene flinched.

"They were waiting," Adrian muttered, ducking away from the window as a return shot splintered the frame beside him. "Goddamn it."

Selene's stomach clenched. "How many?"

Adrian exhaled through his nose, his mind working at lightning speed. "Two that I can see. Maybe more in the shadows." His gaze snapped to hers. "We can't stay here."

No argument there.

Selene scrambled to her feet, careful to avoid the broken glass as Adrian moved toward her. His presence was overwhelming—drenched in rain, in adrenaline, in something else that made her breath catch.

"Follow me," he said.

Selene didn't hesitate.

Adrian led her toward the back of the apartment, his steps silent despite the urgency in the air. He moved like a man who had done this before—who had lived in the margins of danger long enough to know exactly how to escape it.

Selene's fingers curled into fists as she tried to steady her breathing. This wasn't real. It couldn't be real.

She had spent years rebuilding herself, shaping her life into something stable, something safe.

But safety had been an illusion.

And now, that illusion was in flames.

Adrian stopped near the hallway closet, pressing his palm flat against a section of the wall.

Selene frowned. "What are you—"

A click.

The wall shifted, revealing a narrow, hidden passage.

Selene's breath hitched. "Are you serious?"

Adrian didn't give her time to process. "Move."

She did.

The passage was narrow, barely wide enough for them to move side by side, the walls closing in with a quiet, suffocating intensity.

Selene swallowed hard as Adrian shut the hidden door behind them, sealing them into silence. Only the sound of their breathing filled the small space.

She turned to him. "How the hell did you know about this?"

Adrian's expression was unreadable. "Because I made sure it was here."

A chill crawled up her spine. "What?"

His gaze met hers, steady, unflinching. "I had this apartment built with an exit route. In case things ever went south."

Selene's stomach twisted. "You planned for this?"

Adrian exhaled, raking a hand through his damp hair. "Not exactly this."

She stared at him, heart hammering. "You knew something like this would happen. Even back then."

Adrian didn't answer. He didn't have to.

The truth was written all over his face.

A storm of emotions crashed through her. Anger. Fear. Betrayal. And beneath it all, something else—something she didn't want to name.

"Come on," he murmured, his voice quieter now. "This leads to an alleyway two blocks over. If we move fast, we can lose them."

Selene didn't have another choice.

They moved in tense silence, the passage twisting and turning until it finally opened into the cold night air.

The rain had slowed, turning into a light drizzle that made the street slick and shimmering under the glow of the streetlamps. Adrian led the way, his gaze scanning every shadow, every corner.

Selene followed, her pulse a steady roar in her ears.

And then—

A whisper of movement.

Adrian reacted instantly, shoving Selene against the wall, shielding her with his body as a figure stepped out of the darkness.

A man. Tall, dressed in black, his face obscured by the brim of his hood. But there was no mistaking the glint of the gun in his hand.

Selene's breath hitched.

Adrian didn't hesitate.

Smoke and Secrets

In a blur of motion, he lunged.

The struggle was fast, brutal. Adrian twisted the attacker's arm, forcing the gun downward just as a shot rang out, the bullet lodging harmlessly into the pavement.

Selene barely had time to react before Adrian grabbed the man by the collar and slammed him against the wall.

"Who sent you?" Adrian's voice was a low growl, edged with barely contained fury.

The man coughed, his head snapping back against the bricks, but he didn't answer.

Adrian pressed the barrel of his own gun beneath the man's chin.

"I won't ask again."

Selene shivered. She had never seen Adrian like this before—not this version of him, honed by darkness, by survival.

The man let out a raspy chuckle. "You think you can stop them?"

Adrian's grip tightened. "Who?"

The man smirked. "You already know."

Selene's stomach twisted.

Adrian exhaled sharply, then, with a swift movement, knocked the man unconscious.

Selene let out the breath she hadn't realized she was holding.

Adrian turned to her, his expression grim. "We need to move."

Selene nodded, but as they stepped away, her mind was spinning.

The gallery. The letter. The attack.

And now this.

Whoever they were up against, they weren't just coming after Adrian.

They were coming for her.

And this time, there would be no warning shot.

Six

Dancing with the Enemy

The rhythmic thump of bass reverberated through the walls, a pulsing heartbeat that set the tone for the night. Golden chandeliers hung high above the ballroom, casting a warm glow over the sea of people swathed in expensive fabrics and dripping in wealth. The scent of perfume, cigars, and aged whiskey lingered in the air, mingling with the whispers of secrets passed between lips hidden behind crystal glasses.

Selene stepped through the grand entrance of the gala, her pulse steady despite the storm raging inside her. The silk of her dress, deep midnight blue, clung to her in all the right ways, the slit high enough to allow ease of movement, the neckline dangerously elegant.

She was playing a role tonight.

A woman with nothing to fear. A woman who belonged in this world of power, deception, and carefully masked intentions.

Adrian was close behind her, a shadow at her back.

She could feel him without looking—the heat of his body, the barely-there brush of his fingers against the small of her back as they moved deeper into the room. He was dressed in a tailored black suit, sharp and unforgiving, a man built to command attention yet skilled enough to slip through the cracks unseen.

He had warned her against coming.

"You don't understand the kind of people who will be here."

But Selene was done sitting on the sidelines, done being a target without knowing who was pulling the trigger.

This was where they would find answers.

This was where the enemy lurked, smiling behind polished masks.

A waiter passed by with a tray of champagne flutes. Selene plucked one from the silver surface, the stem cold between her fingers as she lifted it to her lips—not to drink, but to complete the illusion. She let her gaze sweep across the room, cataloging faces, searching for something—someone—who felt out of place.

"See anyone you recognize?" Adrian's voice was low, just for her.

Selene exhaled slowly. "Not yet."

"Then let's keep it that way."

His tone was dark, edged with something she couldn't quite name.

Selene turned slightly, just enough for her lips to brush the rim of the glass. "Are you worried about me, Adrian?"

His gaze flickered down to her, and even in the dim, golden light, she saw the tension in his jaw, the way his fingers flexed at his side.

"I'm worried about who might recognize you."

There was something in his voice—something possessive, something protective—that sent a shiver down her spine.

But before she could respond, a voice cut through the space between them.

"Ms. Duvall."

Selene turned, schooling her expression into one of polite curiosity.

A man stood before her, dapper in a navy suit, a silver watch glinting beneath the cuff of his sleeve. He was older, perhaps late fifties, with graying hair swept back from a strong, confident face. But it was his eyes that unsettled her—dark and sharp, like a predator that had already decided his next move.

"I was beginning to wonder if you'd be attending tonight," he said smoothly, extending a hand. "Alexander Graves."

Selene accepted the handshake, her grip firm, betraying nothing.

"Mr. Graves," she replied. "I wasn't aware I had been expected."

His smile was practiced. "Oh, you'd be surprised how much interest your gallery fire has sparked among certain circles."

Her pulse spiked.

The words were a test. A way to measure her reaction.

Selene forced herself to tilt her head slightly, lips curving into a half-smile. "Tragic, isn't it?" she mused, voice laced with casual detachment. "And yet, insurance has been remarkably understanding."

Graves chuckled, as if she had just told an amusing joke. "Yes, well… some tragedies are merely preludes to bigger stories."

Adrian shifted beside her, his presence a steady anchor, though his body had gone rigid.

Selene knew what he was thinking.

This man knows something.

She could feel it too.

"Tell me, Mr. Graves," Selene continued, voice smooth. "Are you in the business of predicting tragedies?"

Graves took a sip from his whiskey glass, his gaze never leaving hers.

"Not predicting," he murmured. "Just observing."

A challenge. A game of subtext and hidden threats.

Adrian took a subtle step forward, placing himself slightly between them, his movement barely perceptible to anyone who wasn't paying attention. But Selene felt it—the silent warning, the unspoken promise in the tension between his shoulder blades.

Graves chuckled, amused. "And you must be Adrian Vale."

Selene felt Adrian stiffen beside her.

Graves turned fully to him, offering the same handshake he had given Selene. Adrian didn't move.

"A ghost," Graves continued, voice low. "Yet here you are. Alive."

Adrian's lips curled into something that wasn't quite a smile. "Disappointed?"

Graves let out another chuckle, shaking his head. "Not at all. Quite the opposite, in fact. It's always fascinating when people who shouldn't exist return to the stage."

The air was heavy, thick with unspoken things.

Selene glanced around the room. No one was paying them any mind. The crowd was still dancing, still drinking, still laughing.

But this conversation—this moment—was anything but casual.

Graves finished the last sip of his whiskey, setting the glass aside.

"I do hope you enjoy the evening," he said, the words meant for both of them. "It would be such a shame if this were your last."

A warning.

A promise.

Selene felt the chill of it crawl over her skin.

And then, Graves turned, disappearing into the crowd like a ghost himself.

She exhaled sharply, forcing her grip to loosen around her champagne flute before it shattered between her fingers.

Adrian leaned in, his voice barely above a whisper.

"We need to leave."

Selene swallowed hard. "Not yet."

Adrian's hand found her waist—not a caress, but a steadying touch, grounding her. "Selene—"

"I need to know what he knows," she insisted.

Adrian's fingers tightened slightly, and for a moment, she wasn't sure if it was out of frustration or something else—something darker, something more possessive.

"You're playing a dangerous game," he murmured, voice low and lethal.

Selene turned her head slightly, just enough so that when she looked up at him, their lips were a breath apart.

"I don't have a choice," she whispered.

Something flared in Adrian's eyes. Something wild.

The air between them crackled, the tension thick enough to choke on.

For a moment, the gala, the danger, the world around them faded, narrowing down to this—to the heat between them, to the gravity pulling them together despite everything.

And then—

A hand brushed her shoulder.

Selene turned, startled.

A new man had joined them.

"I believe this dance is mine," he said, extending a hand toward her.

Selene barely contained her surprise.

But Adrian—Adrian didn't move.

His jaw tightened, his fingers flexing against her waist before, reluctantly, he let her go.

Selene swallowed past the tightness in her throat.

She took the stranger's hand.

And as she was led toward the dance floor, her heart pounded with the truth she couldn't ignore.

She was now dancing with the enemy.

Seven

Shattered Promises

The stranger's fingers closed around Selene's hand—firm, cool, and steady, as if he had done this a thousand times before. As if he had spent years perfecting the art of control.

The moment he led her onto the dance floor, Selene felt the shift. The room was still alive with laughter, the clinking of glasses, the murmurs of power-laced conversations. But here, beneath the glow of the chandeliers and within the embrace of the enemy, everything narrowed to a single, pulsing moment.

The music swelled—a haunting melody laced with something almost mournful.

He guided her with a practiced ease, one hand at the small of her back, the other clasping her palm. His movements were deliberate, effortless, and yet every step felt like a threat wrapped in silk.

Selene's pulse thrummed.

"Ms. Duvall," the man murmured, his voice just above a whisper. "I must admit, I didn't expect you to be quite so bold."

His smile was polite, but his grip was just a fraction too tight, his touch lingering in a way that made her skin crawl.

Selene lifted her chin, meeting his gaze without flinching. "I suppose I never saw the appeal in being predictable."

The man chuckled, his breath warm against her cheek as they spun together, his hold forcing her closer than she would have liked. "No, I imagine you wouldn't."

Selene tried to keep her breathing even, tried not to show how acutely aware she was of Adrian watching from the sidelines, his gaze burning into her.

The man dipped his head slightly, his lips brushing the shell of her ear. "You should be careful, though."

Selene's fingers twitched in his grip, but she didn't pull away. "Is that a warning?"

His smile never wavered, but his eyes darkened. "It's a courtesy."

The words sent a shiver down her spine.

Selene had danced with liars before. She had spent years pretending, mastering the delicate art of deception when necessary. But this—this was different. This man, whoever he was, knew something.

He knew who she was.

And worse—he knew why she was here.

Adrian had been right. She was in over her head.

But it was too late to stop now.

Selene forced herself to exhale, keeping her expression smooth, unreadable. "You seem to know an awful lot about me."

The man's fingers flexed slightly against her spine. "I make it my business to know things."

The music shifted into something slower, more hypnotic. Around them, couples swayed in perfect rhythm, lost in their own worlds.

Selene felt like she was dancing on the edge of a blade.

"And what else do you know?" she asked, tilting her head just enough to watch his reaction.

His smile never faltered, but his grip did. Just barely.

Enough for her to know she had hit something.

"I know that Adrian Vale was a fool to leave you behind," he said smoothly.

The words sent a jolt through her, quick and sharp.

Selene forced herself not to react.

He was baiting her.

She refused to take it.

"Is that so?" she murmured, keeping her voice neutral.

The man chuckled. "Oh, don't misunderstand. He had his reasons, I'm sure." His thumb brushed lightly over her hand as he turned her in a slow, calculated spin. "But men like him never truly leave. Do they?"

Selene's breath hitched.

She knew then—he wasn't just testing her. He was testing Adrian.

This was a game of pressure points, of weaknesses revealed through the smallest cracks.

And Adrian, despite all his efforts, had left a crack wide enough for the enemy to slip through.

Selene narrowed her eyes. "If you wanted to talk about Adrian, you could have done it over a drink."

The man smirked. "Ah, but where's the fun in that?"

She was running out of patience.

"Who are you?" she demanded.

His smirk faded slightly, his fingers tightening around hers. "You already know the answer."

Selene's stomach twisted.

Alexander Graves had been a warning.

This man was a message.

A statement.

She wasn't just being watched.

She was being studied.

Then, just as quickly as the tension thickened between them, the man released her. The music swelled to its crescendo, and he took a step back, bowing his head slightly.

"A pleasure, Ms. Duvall," he murmured.

Selene swallowed hard, her fingers still tingling where he had touched her.

Before she could speak, he was gone, disappearing into the sea of people, swallowed whole by the crowd.

A hand grabbed her wrist.

Adrian.

His grip was firm, his expression a storm barely contained beneath the surface.

"What the hell was that?" he growled, pulling her toward the farthest edge of the room, away from prying eyes.

Selene yanked free. "I was gathering information."

Adrian's jaw clenched. "He wasn't gathering information. He was studying you."

Selene exhaled sharply. "I know."

Adrian's fingers flexed at his sides, his frustration barely contained. "Then why didn't you walk away?"

Selene met his gaze head-on. "Because I needed to know what we're up against."

Adrian let out a rough breath, running a hand through his hair. "You don't even realize how dangerous this is."

Selene took a step closer. "Then tell me, Adrian. Tell me what you're so afraid of."

His eyes darkened. "I'm afraid of you ending up like me."

Selene stilled.

The words hit harder than she expected.

For the first time since he had come back, she saw it—the weight he carried, the ghosts that followed him.

She softened. Just slightly.

"I need to do this," she said quietly.

Adrian's throat bobbed, his expression torn.

Then, in one swift motion, he stepped closer, crowding into her space, his breath hot against her skin.

"I need you alive more."

Selene's breath caught.

Adrian's hand came up, fingers grazing her jaw, his touch light but dangerous.

This was the edge of something they shouldn't be standing on.

But neither of them moved.

Neither of them looked away.

Then—

A sharp sound.

Not a gunshot.

Not a scream.

A crackling noise—unnatural, electric.

And then—

The ballroom lights flickered.

For a second, the world stood still.

Then, everything went black.

Selene's pulse roared.

The darkness swallowed the room whole, and just as the chaos began—just as the first panicked voices rose around them—Selene felt Adrian's arm wrap around her waist.

"We need to go," he whispered against her ear.

But before they could move—

A whisper.

Close.

Shattered Promises

Too close.

And then—

A voice in the dark.

"Some flames should die."

The words slithered through the void like a promise.

Selene's blood ran cold.

And then, just as quickly as the lights had gone out—

They came back on.

Selene turned—spinning, searching.

But whoever had spoken was already gone.

And the world, for one brief, aching moment—

Felt smaller than ever.

Eight

A Trail of Ash and Lies

Selene's pulse roared in her ears, drowning out the distant murmur of guests as the gala's lights flickered back to life. The world around her reassembled itself in fragments—glowing chandeliers, swirling gowns, murmured confusion. But her mind was fixed on only one thing.

Some flames should die.

The whisper still clung to the air, thick as smoke. The weight of those words pressed against her chest, colder than the night outside. Someone had been close. Too close.

Adrian's hand was still wrapped around her waist, grounding her in place. His grip was firm, protective. She could feel the tension in his muscles, the barely controlled fury simmering beneath his composed exterior.

"Did you hear that?" she murmured, her voice tight with the aftermath of fear.

Adrian's jaw clenched. "Yes."

He was already scanning the room, his sharp gaze flicking over every shadowed figure, every lingering guest whose expression showed more curiosity than alarm. No one else seemed to have noticed the whispered threat. It had been meant only for them.

Adrian's grip tightened briefly before he released her. "We're leaving. Now."

Selene hesitated, her eyes searching the crowd, desperate for something—anything—that would give her a clue as to who had whispered those chilling words. But all she found were unfamiliar faces, masks of wealth and power, painted smiles that concealed far too much.

She turned back to Adrian, her own voice a whisper now. "Do you think it was Graves?"

Adrian exhaled sharply. "No. Graves wouldn't be so... subtle. Whoever that was, they didn't want an audience."

That thought unsettled her even more.

A whisper meant a warning.

A warning meant they were running out of time.

Adrian grabbed her hand, his fingers lacing briefly through hers before he let go, ushering her toward the side exit. His movements were precise, controlled. To anyone watching, they were just another couple slipping away from the gala early.

But Selene could feel it.

The weight of eyes on her back.

The silent promise that they weren't alone.

The night air hit like a shock of cold water as they stepped outside, the heavy door shutting behind them with an eerie finality. The gala's distant hum faded, replaced by the steady rhythm of raindrops tapping against pavement.

Selene wrapped her arms around herself, shivering as Adrian led her swiftly down a narrow alleyway, away from the grand estate and the watching eyes within it.

He didn't stop until they reached the sleek black car waiting at the curb. Without a word, he opened the passenger door for her.

Selene hesitated, looking up at him. "Where are we going?"

Adrian's expression was unreadable. "Somewhere safe."

Selene let out a hollow laugh. "Safe? You keep saying that, but nowhere has been safe since the moment you came back."

Adrian flinched. It was brief—so brief she might have imagined it.

Then, without another word, he shut the door behind her.

The car's interior was cool, the leather seats smooth beneath her fingertips as she exhaled, trying to steady herself. Adrian slid into the driver's seat, his hands gripping the wheel as he stared straight ahead.

For a long moment, neither of them spoke.

Selene broke the silence first. "That wasn't a coincidence, was it?"

Adrian's knuckles whitened against the wheel. "No."

Selene swallowed hard. "Then what does it mean?"

Adrian finally turned to look at her, his gaze dark, unreadable. "It means they know you're part of this now."

Selene felt the weight of those words settle deep in her chest. They. The faceless, nameless threat that had been circling her like a predator in the dark.

She exhaled shakily, pressing her fingertips against her temples. "Why? What do they want?"

Adrian hesitated. Just long enough for her to notice.

Selene's stomach twisted. "You know something," she accused.

Adrian's jaw tensed. "I don't have all the answers."

"But you have some," she shot back. "So stop protecting me and start telling me the truth."

Adrian sighed, running a hand through his hair before finally speaking. "They don't just want me dead, Selene. They want to erase everything tied to me."

Selene frowned. "Erase?"

Adrian turned to face her fully now, his expression grim. "My past. The people I knew. The people I loved."

The words hung between them, heavy and unspoken.

The people I loved.

Selene's throat went dry.

"They think I know something. Something I shouldn't." Adrian's voice was quiet, controlled. "And if they think you're important to me..." His fingers curled into fists. "Then you become leverage."

Selene let out a slow breath. Leverage.

She should have felt anger. Should have resented the fact that she was caught in this web because of him.

But all she felt was fear.

Not for herself.

For him.

She looked at him then, really looked at him—the tension in his shoulders, the exhaustion in his eyes, the weight of years spent running, fighting, losing.

Selene swallowed hard, her voice softer now. "You're scared."

Adrian stiffened.

Selene reached for his hand before she could think better of it, her fingers brushing over his knuckles. He flinched, but he didn't pull away.

She traced the faint scars along his skin, the ghosts of battles he had never spoken about. "I know you, Adrian," she whispered. "I know when you're lying. And I know when you're afraid."

His throat bobbed.

For a moment, just a fleeting second, the mask cracked.

Adrian exhaled, his fingers twitching beneath hers. "I can't lose you again."

Selene's heart twisted painfully.

Three years of silence. Three years of grief. Three years of never knowing.

And yet here they were.

His words weren't a declaration.

They were a confession.

And Selene hated how much she still wanted to believe in them.

She squeezed his hand, grounding herself. "Then stop running."

Adrian let out a bitter laugh. "I don't know how."

Selene's grip tightened. "Then let me show you."

For a moment, neither of them moved.

Then—slowly, carefully—Adrian lifted their joined hands, pressing his lips to the inside of her wrist. The touch was light, barely there. A whisper of something that had once been everything.

Selene's breath hitched.

He pulled away before she could speak, his voice hoarse. "We have to keep moving."

Selene nodded, even as her pulse thundered in her veins.

The moment had passed.

But something between them had shifted.

And this time—

There would be no going back.

Nine

The Edge of Betrayal

The city blurred past them, neon lights streaking across the wet pavement as Adrian weaved through the streets with a precision that spoke of years spent running from danger. Rain pelted the windshield, each drop a frantic whisper against the glass, and Selene couldn't shake the feeling that they were being swallowed by the night itself.

She had stopped asking where they were going miles ago.

Adrian's grip on the steering wheel was tight, his knuckles white with the kind of tension that sent a shiver down her spine. His jaw was clenched, and his eyes—those dark, haunted eyes—were fixed on the road, scanning, always scanning.

He hadn't spoken since they left the gala.

Neither had she.

The weight of what had happened—of the whisper in the dark, of the truth Adrian had finally admitted—still clung to her skin, cold and suffocating.

She knew now.

She was leverage.

They would use her to break him, to drag him back into whatever hell he had crawled out of, and Adrian—for all his secrets, for all his lies—was terrified of that.

She should have been angry.

She should have felt something other than this awful, twisted ache in her chest.

But all she could think about was the way he had looked at her, the way his fingers had lingered against hers, the way his lips had brushed her wrist as if he were trying to memorize the feeling.

Selene exhaled sharply, breaking the silence.

"Are we going to talk about it?"

Adrian didn't flinch. "Talk about what?"

She narrowed her eyes. "Don't do that. Don't pretend like none of this is happening."

His grip on the wheel tightened. "None of this should be happening."

Selene let out a sharp, humorless laugh. "And yet, here we are."

Adrian's jaw tensed, but he said nothing.

Selene turned to face him fully. "You said they think I'm important to you."

He exhaled slowly, carefully. "You are."

The words settled between them like a live wire, crackling and charged.

Selene swallowed, her throat dry. "Then tell me, Adrian. What happens now?"

A muscle in his jaw ticked. "I get you out of this."

Selene shook her head. "That's not an answer. That's an excuse to keep shutting me out."

The car jerked slightly as Adrian's hands tightened on the wheel. "I don't have time for this."

"Make time," she shot back, her voice laced with frustration. "Because I am done letting you decide what I get to know."

Adrian exhaled sharply, but before he could respond, the car's headlights caught a flicker of movement up ahead.

Selene saw it at the same time he did.

A black SUV. Parked across the street, blocking their path.

Her stomach dropped.

Adrian's reaction was instant. He slammed his foot against the brake, the tires screeching as the car skidded to a stop. Selene's breath caught as the seatbelt yanked her back, her heart hammering.

The street was empty. Too empty.

It was a trap.

Adrian cursed under his breath.

Then, before Selene could process what was happening, he threw the car into reverse.

The tires screeched as they lurched backward, but before they could gain enough distance, another set of headlights flared to life in the rearview mirror.

Another SUV.

Selene's pulse skyrocketed.

They were boxed in.

Adrian muttered something under his breath that sounded a lot like goddamn it before he reached into the glove compartment and pulled out a gun.

Selene's stomach clenched. "Adrian—"

"Stay low," he ordered, voice razor-sharp.

Selene's breath came in short, shallow bursts as she pressed herself against the seat, her mind racing.

The SUV doors opened.

Four men stepped out, their silhouettes dark against the glow of the streetlights.

Selene couldn't see their faces, but she didn't need to.

Everything about them—the way they moved, the way they held themselves—screamed military precision.

Adrian's grip tightened on the gun.

"Don't move," he murmured.

Selene didn't.

Her fingers curled into fists as she watched one of the men step forward, his posture eerily calm.

Adrian lowered the window slightly, just enough to speak. "You're making a mistake."

The man let out a quiet chuckle. "Am I?"

Selene's skin prickled.

That voice.

She knew that voice.

Her pulse spiked as the man stepped fully into the glow of the headlights.

It wasn't just a stranger.

It was someone she had met before.

Someone who had danced with her at the gala.

Selene's blood ran cold.

"You," she whispered.

The man smiled, slow and deliberate. "You remember me. Good."

Adrian's body was coiled with tension, his fingers flexing against the grip of the gun. "Who sent you?"

The man tilted his head slightly, as if amused. "Do you really need to ask?"

Selene's stomach twisted. Graves.

Of course.

Adrian exhaled through his nose. "You know how this ends."

The man's smile didn't falter. "That depends. Are you willing to negotiate?"

Adrian didn't respond.

The silence stretched, thick and suffocating.

Then, without warning, Adrian lifted the gun.

Selene barely had time to react before a shot rang out.

Not Adrian's.

The man had fired first.

The bullet shattered the driver's side window, glass exploding inward. Selene flinched as shards sliced across her skin, her heart slamming against her ribs.

Adrian didn't hesitate.

With a sharp movement, he kicked open the door, using it as a shield as he fired back.

Chaos erupted.

Selene ducked, adrenaline surging as more shots rang out.

"Selene, run!" Adrian shouted.

Her body moved before her mind caught up.

She threw open the door, sprinting toward the nearest alleyway. Her heels slipped against the rain-slick pavement, but she didn't stop.

She could hear Adrian behind her, the sound of footsteps closing in.

Then—

A hand grabbed her wrist.

She yelped, twisting instinctively, but the grip was unrelenting.

She turned—expecting one of the men—

But it was Adrian.

His chest was heaving, his eyes wild.

"We need to split up," he rasped.

Selene shook her head. "No."

"Selene—"

"I am not leaving you."

Adrian exhaled sharply, his grip tightening before—to her shock—he pulled her against him.

His lips crushed against hers, hard and desperate, as if this was the only chance he'd ever have.

The world tilted.

Selene's fingers curled into his jacket, clinging to him as his hands cupped her face, his body pressed against hers like he was afraid to let go.

Then—

He pulled away, his forehead pressing against hers for just a moment.

"I'll find you," he promised.

Then, before she could stop him—before she could tell him she didn't want to be found without him—he was gone.

Disappearing into the night like a shadow.

And Selene—breathless, shaken—was left standing in the rain, knowing this was just the beginning.

Ten

Flames of the Past

The night swallowed Selene whole.

She ran.

Rain slicked the pavement beneath her feet, the distant city lights flickering like dying embers as she darted through the alleyway, her breath ragged, her heart hammering against her ribs. Each footstep felt like a countdown, each shadow a threat lurking just beyond her vision.

Adrian was gone.

The echo of his kiss still burned against her lips, raw and desperate, a silent promise that felt too much like a farewell.

Her fingers curled into fists as she forced herself to move faster.

She had to get out of here.

Somewhere behind her, voices cut through the rain—sharp, clipped orders. The men who had ambushed them weren't giving up easily. They weren't just after Adrian.

They wanted her.

Selene turned a corner sharply, slipping against the wet ground, her breath coming in short bursts. She had no idea where she was going—only that she had to keep moving.

Then—a flicker of light.

Up ahead, a neon sign buzzed faintly, casting an eerie red glow onto the rain-soaked street.

A bar.

It was open.

Without thinking, she pushed through the door, the warm scent of whiskey and stale cigarettes hitting her as she stumbled inside. The noise of the city was muffled here, replaced by the low hum of conversation, the clinking of glasses, the scratchy sound of an old blues song playing from the jukebox.

The bartender—a man in his sixties with a weathered face and eyes that had seen too much—glanced up from where he was cleaning a glass.

Selene took a steadying breath, forcing herself to blend in.

She walked toward the bar, ignoring the curious glances from a few scattered patrons. The weight of her drenched clothes made her shiver, but she fought against the exhaustion pressing down on her.

She slid into a barstool, fingers gripping the worn wood.

The bartender raised a brow. "Rough night?"

Selene let out a breathless laugh. "Something like that."

The man studied her for a moment before nodding. "What'll it be?"

She hesitated. "Whiskey. Neat."

The bartender poured the drink without another word, setting the glass in front of her. Selene wrapped her fingers around it, the warmth seeping into her chilled skin.

She didn't drink it.

Instead, she let her gaze flicker toward the entrance, her reflection barely visible in the rain-streaked window.

The street outside was empty.

For now.

She knew better than to think they had given up.

She needed to disappear.

A movement to her right caught her attention.

A man had slid onto the stool beside her, silent as a ghost.

Selene's pulse spiked.

She turned slowly, her fingers tightening around the glass.

The man wasn't one of Graves' men. She would've recognized him instantly if he were.

But that didn't mean he wasn't dangerous.

He was in his mid-forties, dressed in a charcoal suit that looked too sharp for a place like this. His hair was neatly combed back, streaked with silver at the temples, and his eyes—dark and unreadable—were already on her.

Selene forced herself to stay still. "Can I help you?"

The man smiled faintly. "I was just about to ask you the same thing."

Her stomach clenched.

She set her drink down carefully. "I'm not looking for company."

The man tilted his head slightly. "A woman like you, alone, in a place like this?" His voice was smooth, deliberate. "You're either very brave or very stupid."

Selene smiled, but there was no warmth in it. "Maybe I'm both."

The man chuckled. "Fair enough."

For a moment, neither of them spoke.

Then—

"I saw what happened outside," he said, his voice casual. "Seemed like you were in a hurry to get away from something."

Selene's pulse kicked up a notch. "You must be mistaken."

The man leaned in slightly. "Don't insult me. I know who you are, Selene Duvall."

Every muscle in her body went rigid.

She did not react.

Did not blink.

Did not let the panic clawing at her chest show on her face.

The man took a sip of his drink, as if completely unaffected by the shift in tension.

"I can help you," he said.

Selene scoffed. "Right. Because men who track me down in dive bars always have my best interests at heart."

The man chuckled. "Touché."

Selene exhaled slowly. "Who are you?"

The man set his glass down, turning fully toward her. "Let's just say I used to work with Adrian."

A chill ran down her spine.

The man smiled. "Now I have your attention."

Selene's heart hammered. "Why should I believe you?"

"Because if I wanted to turn you in, you wouldn't be sitting here right now."

She hated that he had a point.

The man leaned in slightly. "Adrian's in trouble. Real trouble."

Selene's throat tightened. "I know."

The man shook his head. "No. You don't."

Selene's fingers curled against the bar. "Then tell me."

The man exhaled. "Three years ago, Adrian wasn't just running from Graves. He was running from everyone. He uncovered something—something he wasn't supposed to. And now, they want to erase everything."

Selene's stomach twisted. "What did he find?"

The man's gaze darkened. "The truth."

A sharp crack of thunder echoed outside, rattling the windows.

Selene forced herself to breathe.

The truth.

The reason Adrian had disappeared.

The reason people were still trying to kill him.

She swallowed past the tightness in her throat. "And what do you want?"

The man's expression was unreadable. "To finish what Adrian started."

Selene studied him. "And what does that mean for me?"

The man smiled faintly. "That depends."

Selene's skin prickled. "On what?"

The man leaned back slightly. "On whether you're ready to stop being a pawn and start being a player."

The words settled between them, heavy and deliberate.

Selene exhaled slowly.

She thought of Adrian.

Of the way he had looked at her before he disappeared into the night.

Of the ghosts that haunted his eyes.

She thought of the fire. The whispers in the dark.

And she knew.

She wasn't running anymore.

She was hunting.

Selene met the man's gaze, her decision made.

"Tell me everything."

Eleven

When Fire Meets Fire

S elene had always believed there was a moment—just before everything shattered—where time slowed. Where the world inhaled sharply before the fall.

She felt it now.

Sitting in the dimly lit back room of the bar, the air thick with cigarette smoke and old secrets, she listened to the man across from her spin a story of betrayal, power, and a war waged in the shadows.

His name was Marcus Hale, and he knew too much.

The table between them was small, but it felt like a chasm. A battlefield where words were weapons and every revelation was another step closer to the edge.

Selene curled her fingers around her glass, the whiskey inside untouched, her pulse a steady drumbeat against her ribs.

"Start from the beginning," she said, voice steady despite the storm unraveling inside her.

Marcus studied her for a long moment before leaning back in his chair. His fingers drummed against the table, calculating.

Then, he spoke.

"Three years ago, Adrian wasn't just running from Graves," Marcus said, his voice low, even. "He was running from something bigger. Something that didn't want to be seen."

Selene's stomach twisted.

She knew this already. She had suspected it. But hearing it confirmed—**hearing that Adrian had been hunted not just by Graves, but by something far worse—**made the room feel colder.

Marcus continued, his gaze sharp. "Adrian was part of something once. A group embedded deep in the underbelly of this city. They weren't just criminals. They weren't just spies. They were something... more."

Selene exhaled, her fingers tightening around the glass. "A syndicate."

Marcus's lips curved slightly. "Clever girl."

When Fire Meets Fire

Selene ignored the chill running down her spine. "And Adrian was part of it."

Marcus nodded. "Until he became a problem."

Selene's throat went dry.

She leaned forward. "What did he find?"

Marcus hesitated. Just for a moment.

Then—

"He found proof that the syndicate wasn't just dealing in secrets. They were dealing in people."

The words landed like a gunshot.

Selene's mind reeled.

She had expected something—money laundering, blackmail, even assassinations.

But this?

This was something worse.

Something far worse.

Marcus's expression darkened. "Women. Children. Anyone who could be used, bought, sold. Adrian found evidence—proof that they were operating on a global scale, trafficking people like they were commodities."

Selene felt the bile rise in her throat.

Adrian had found this.

And suddenly, his disappearance made sense.

Selene swallowed hard. "He tried to stop them."

Marcus nodded. "And they made him disappear."

A heavy silence settled between them.

Selene exhaled slowly, her thoughts racing. This was the truth.

The reason Adrian had vanished.

The reason he had let her believe he was dead.

Her pulse pounded.

Marcus studied her, his dark gaze unreadable. "They think Adrian still has something. Some piece of evidence he kept for himself. That's why they want him dead."

Selene's fingers curled into fists. "Then why are they after me?"

Marcus's jaw tightened.

When he spoke, his voice was quieter. "Because they think he gave it to you."

Selene stilled.

Her breath caught.

And suddenly, everything—**the fire, the threats, the way Adrian had tried to push her away—**made sense.

They weren't just after Adrian.

They thought she had the proof.

Selene exhaled sharply, pressing her palms against the table.

"I don't," she said. "I don't have anything."

Marcus tilted his head slightly. "Maybe. Maybe not. But they don't believe that. And until they do, you're in just as much danger as he is."

Selene swallowed hard.

A sharp, aching pressure built behind her ribs.

She had spent years trying to rebuild her life, thinking Adrian had left her in the dark. Thinking he had abandoned her.

But now—now she knew.

He had been protecting her all along.

Selene took a steadying breath. "Where is he?"

Marcus leaned back, considering her. "Why?"

Selene's jaw tightened. "Because I'm not running anymore."

Marcus exhaled, watching her carefully. "He won't let you do this."

Selene let out a humorless laugh. "Then he'll just have to try and stop me."

A flicker of something passed through Marcus's expression—respect, maybe. Amusement.

Then, finally—

"I can take you to him."

Selene's pulse spiked.

She met his gaze. "Then let's go."

The warehouse smelled like rust and rain.

Selene's footsteps were silent as she followed Marcus through the darkened corridors, the dim light casting long shadows against the concrete walls.

Adrian was here.

She felt it.

Her body hummed with awareness, her breath uneven as Marcus led her deeper into the maze of abandoned steel and broken glass.

Then—

A door.

Marcus stopped. Turned to her.

"This is your last chance to walk away."

Selene didn't hesitate. "Open it."

Marcus nodded.

He pushed the door open.

And there—

Standing in the center of the room, his back to her, his hands braced against an old metal table—

Was Adrian.

Selene's breath hitched.

The moment he heard the door, he turned—and the second his eyes met hers, the world tilted.

She barely had time to process before he was in front of her, gripping her arms, his expression a mix of fury, relief, and something dangerously close to desperation.

"What the hell are you doing here?"

Selene exhaled sharply, meeting his gaze.

"Saving you."

Adrian cursed under his breath. His grip on her arms was firm, his body radiating heat, tension. "You shouldn't have come."

Selene lifted her chin. "I didn't come alone."

Adrian's gaze flicked to Marcus, sharp as a blade.

"What did you tell her?"

Marcus smirked. "Everything."

Adrian's fingers tightened on her arms. "Selene—"

She cut him off. "No. No more secrets. No more running."

Adrian exhaled sharply. "You don't know what you've done."

Selene's heart pounded. "I know exactly what I've done."

When Fire Meets Fire

And then, before she could say another word—

A gunshot.

The door behind them exploded inward.

Selene barely had time to react before Adrian grabbed her, shielding her with his body as bullets tore through the room.

Marcus was already moving, returning fire, his expression grim.

"They found us!"

Selene's pulse skyrocketed.

Adrian's grip on her was unyielding. His voice was rough, urgent.

"We need to get out of here. Now."

Selene swallowed past the fear clawing at her throat.

She had come here for Adrian.

And now, they were both running for their lives.

But this time—

She wasn't letting go.

Twelve

the Forgotten Flame

Gunfire erupted like a violent storm, ricocheting off steel and concrete and drowning out the frantic pounding of Selene's heart. The sharp scent of gunpowder filled the warehouse air, mingling with rust and rain. She barely had time to react before Adrian yanked her against him, his body shielding hers as another round of bullets tore through the walls.

"Move!" Adrian barked, gripping her wrist and dragging her into the shadows.

Selene stumbled, adrenaline roaring through her veins. The echoes of gunfire sent sparks flying from the metal shelves, cutting through the darkness like firecrackers in a war zone. Marcus was already ahead of them, firing back at the unseen attackers as they pushed deeper into the labyrinth of abandoned storage crates.

A bullet struck dangerously close, shattering the glass of a hanging light fixture. Shards rained down like falling stars, and Selene felt the sting as one grazed her cheek.

She didn't scream.

She wouldn't.

Not now.

Adrian's grip was iron-tight as he pulled her down behind a rusted shipping container, his breaths harsh against her ear. "Stay low," he ordered.

Selene pressed herself against the cold metal, gripping the pistol Adrian had slipped into her hands moments ago. She barely knew how to use it, but that no longer mattered.

She had no choice.

A shadow moved in the periphery of her vision.

Marcus fired. A body hit the ground with a sickening thud.

Selene's stomach twisted, but she didn't flinch.

Adrian peeked over the edge of the container, scanning the darkness. "They're closing in."

Marcus reloaded, his expression grim. "We need to get out before they block the exits."

Adrian cursed under his breath.

Selene swallowed hard. "How many are there?"

"Too many," Marcus muttered.

Adrian exhaled sharply, his eyes locking onto hers. "When I say run, you run. Don't stop. Don't look back. Understand?"

Selene's chest tightened.

No.

Not this.

Not another goodbye wrapped in an order.

"Not without you," she said, her voice unwavering.

Adrian's jaw clenched.

Another round of bullets sprayed overhead, forcing them lower.

They didn't have time for this argument.

Adrian grabbed her face, his fingers framing her jaw with an urgency that stole her breath. His lips crashed against hers, desperate, unrelenting. It wasn't just a kiss—it was everything.

the Forgotten Flame

A battle cry.

A promise.

A goodbye that she refused to accept.

When he pulled away, his forehead rested against hers for a fleeting second. "I'll be right behind you."

Selene searched his eyes. "You better be."

Then—

"Go!"

Selene didn't hesitate.

She pushed off the ground, sprinting through the maze of crates and broken machinery. Her pulse roared, her body moving on instinct. Footsteps pounded behind her. More gunfire.

Adrian was there.

She felt him.

Felt the heat of his presence, the sheer gravity of him even through the chaos.

A man appeared in her path.

Selene didn't think.

She fired.

The gun kicked in her hand, the force rattling up her arms.

The man collapsed.

Her hands shook, but she kept running.

The warehouse exit loomed ahead—a large metal door, partially ajar, swaying in the wind. Freedom.

Almost there.

Almost—

A figure stepped into the doorway.

Selene skidded to a stop, her breath catching in her throat.

Alexander Graves.

Calm. Unruffled. A cigarette dangling between his fingers.

"Leaving so soon?"

Selene raised the gun.

Graves didn't move.

Didn't even blink.

"Go ahead," he said smoothly, taking a slow drag from his cigarette. "Shoot me. See what happens."

Selene's finger trembled on the trigger.

Then—a voice behind her.

"Drop it, Selene."

She froze.

Turned.

Adrian.

Held at gunpoint.

Two men flanked him, their weapons pressed against his ribs.

Selene's stomach dropped.

No.

Not again.

Graves exhaled, letting the smoke curl lazily into the air. "There it is," he murmured. "The fire. The fight. Just like him."

Selene gritted her teeth. "Let him go."

Graves smirked. "That's not how this works, sweetheart."

Her pulse pounded.

Options.

She needed options.

Then—Marcus.

A shadow moving behind the men holding Adrian.

Selene's heart slammed against her ribs.

Distract them.

She took a slow, deliberate step forward. "You don't need him," she said, forcing steel into her voice. "I'm the one you want, aren't I?"

Graves arched a brow. "Are you offering yourself?"

Selene swallowed. "I'm offering you a deal."

Graves chuckled. "You think you're in a position to bargain?"

Marcus struck.

A knife to the throat of the first man. A gunshot to the second.

Adrian moved.

Selene fired.

Chaos.

Graves vanished.

Adrian was at her side, blood splattered across his shirt, his chest rising and falling in ragged breaths.

"Are you okay?" she asked, voice shaking.

He stared at her.

Then, before she could react, he crushed her against him, his arms wrapping so tightly around her she could barely breathe.

"You scared the hell out of me," he murmured into her hair.

Selene's fingers curled into his jacket, holding him just as fiercely.

Marcus cleared his throat. "We need to go. Now."

Adrian pulled back, his hands lingering on her arms.

Selene nodded.

They ran.

The safehouse smelled of dust and old books.

Selene stood by the window, staring at the city lights, trying to process everything.

Adrian was alive.

They had made it.

But Graves was still out there.

A storm still waiting to break.

She felt Adrian before he touched her.

His hands slid around her waist, his body pressing against her back, solid and warm.

She exhaled, leaning into him.

"You should rest," he murmured.

Selene turned in his arms, looking up at him. "So should you."

Adrian's lips quirked slightly. "Can't. Not until I know you're safe."

Selene reached up, brushing a stray lock of hair from his forehead.

"You can't protect me from everything," she whispered.

Adrian exhaled. "Doesn't mean I won't try."

Selene swallowed past the lump in her throat.

She cupped his face, her thumb grazing the rough stubble along his jaw.

Adrian's breath hitched.

Then—slowly—she kissed him.

This time, it wasn't desperate.

It wasn't a goodbye.

It was a beginning.

When they pulled apart, Adrian rested his forehead against hers.

"We're not done yet," he murmured.

Selene's lips curled into a small, determined smile.

"No," she said softly.

"We're just getting started."

www.ingramcontent.com/pod-product-compliance
Lightning Source LLC
LaVergne TN
LVHW010551070526
838199LV00063BA/4940